Visual Geography Series®

# EL SALVADOR
## ...in Pictures

Prepared by
Nathan A. Haverstock

Lerner Publications Company
Minneapolis

Independent Picture Service

**Carrying extra produce in a basket on her head, a
farm woman makes her way to market.**

This is an all-new edition of the Visual Geography
Series. Previous editions have been published by
Sterling Publishing Company, New York City, and
some of the original textual information has been re-
tained. New photographs, maps, charts, captions, and
updated information have been added. The text has
been entirely reset in 10/12 Century Textbook.

LIBRARY OF CONGRESS CATALOGING-IN-PUBLICATION DATA

Haverstock, Nathan A.
  El Salvador in pictures.

  (Visual geography series)
  Includes index.
  Summary: Introduces the geography, history, govern-
ment, people, and economy of the smallest and most
densely populated of the Central American nations.
  1. El Salvador. [1. El Salvador]  I. Title.
II. Series: Visual geography series (Minneapolis, Minn.)
F1483.H38  1987    972.84    86–15379
ISBN 0–8225–1806–6 (lib. bdg.)

International Standard Book Number: 0-8225-1806-6
Library of Congress Catalog Card Number: 86-15379

## VISUAL GEOGRAPHY SERIES ®

**Publisher**
Harry Jonas Lerner
**Associate Publisher**
Nancy M. Campbell
**Executive Series Editor**
Lawrence J. Zwier
**Assistant Series Editor**
Mary M. Rodgers
**Editorial Assistant**
Nora W. Kniskern
**Illustrations Editor**
Nathan A. Haverstock
**Consultants/Contributors**
Dr. Ruth F. Hale
Nathan A. Haverstock
Sandra K. Davis
**Designer**
Jim Simondet
**Cartographer**
Carol F. Barrett
**Indexer**
Kristine S. Schubert
**Production Manager**
Richard J. Hannah

Courtesy of United Nations

**A Salvadoran woman washes clothes in Lake Güija.**

### Acknowledgments

Title page photo courtesy of Earl H. Lubensky.

Elevation contours adapted from *The Times Atlas of
the World*, seventh comprehensive edition (New
York: Times Books, 1985).

3   4   5   6   7   8   9   10   96   95   94   93   92   91   90   89   88

Courtesy of Inter-American Development Bank

Children await the arrival of a truck that will take them to school at the village of Santa Ines. The high population growth rate in El Salvador translates into large families—9 to 14 children is not uncommon, particularly in rural areas.

# Contents

GUATEMALA

HONDURAS

Lake Güija

La Palma

Lempa R.

Chalchuapa

Santa Ana

Cihuatán

CUSCATLAN (Ruins)

TAZUMAL (Ruins)

Ahuachapán

Lake Coatepeque

Sonsonate

Delgado

Cojutepeque

SAN SALVADOR

Tecla

Lake Ilopango

San Vicente

Pan-American Highway

QUELEPA (Ruins)

Acajutla

La Libertad

Zacatecoluca

Lempa R.

San Miguel

Usulután

San Miguel R.

La Unión

Lake Olomega

Gulf of Fonseca

La Paz R.

**N**

# EL SALVADOR

——— Department Boundary

*PACIFIC OCEAN*

| 0 | | | 30 Miles |

| 0 | | | 30 Kilometers |

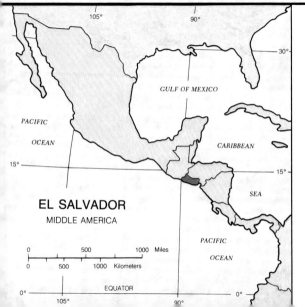

105°    90°

30°

GULF OF MEXICO

PACIFIC OCEAN

CARIBBEAN

15°    15°

SEA

# EL SALVADOR

MIDDLE AMERICA

PACIFIC OCEAN

0    500    1000 Miles

0    500    1000 Kilometers

EQUATOR    0°    0°

105°    90°

Nearly one-fifth of El Salvador's total population lives in the capital city of San Salvador. The crush of people is especially evident at the noon hour—a time of traffic congestion, exhaust fumes, and workers weaving between slow-moving cars.

# Introduction

War-torn, economically depressed, politically divided, overpopulated, mountainous—all these descriptions portray El Salvador, the smallest of the Central American nations.

By the mid-1980s, after several years of civil strife, 60,000 Salvadorans had died. Thirty thousand of these were civilians caught in the crossfire. Nearly one million citizens—one-fifth of the entire population—have fled to safer havens. Roughly 250,000 now reside in neighboring countries of Central America and in Mexico, and a further 300,000 to 600,000 have settled in the United States—with or without the proper entry papers. And the number of refugees rises every day.

El Salvador is the most densely populated nation on the mainland of the Americas—with nearly three times as many people per square mile as the crowded People's Republic of China. Intense pressure on available land resources and a hunger for land are among the causes of the country's historic conflicts. Indeed, the illegal settlement of 300,000 Salvadorans in neighboring Honduras was a major factor in the short-but-bloody 1969 war between the two countries.

For most of the five centuries since the arrival of the Spanish conquistadors, the rural poor of El Salvador have worked the wealth-producing plantations whose profits paid the bills of wasteful governments

5

and of affluent families living in the capital city.

Even today, there are no schools in rural El Salvador for more than 40 percent of children at the primary-school level. Moreover, a Salvadoran child's education—in a country where 46 percent of the total population is 15 years old or less—may end as early as the second grade.

In mid-1988 Salvadorans learned that José Napoleón Duarte—the president of El Salvador since 1984—was seriously ill. This news came at an already difficult period in Duarte's administration. Death squad activities had increased, leaving more victims of politically motivated violence, and inflation was on the rise.

Even if Duarte had not become ill, he could not, according to El Salvador's constitution, run for another term as president. Whether the people choose a Christian

The smoking cone of Izalco Volcano is seen from Lake Coatepeque, one of El Salvador's largest lakes.

Democratic candidate again or a more conservative leader, Salvadorans are determined to remedy the injustices they have endured.

A crowded, poorly equipped, and understaffed classroom in Santa Ines illustrates that public education is woefully lacking in El Salvador, especially in rural areas. Since the outbreak of civil war, fewer Salvadoran children are attending school.

6

A section of the Pan-American Highway makes its arduous journey through the mountainous terrain of El Salvador. Road building was not an easy task, given the steep and rocky landscape that exists throughout the nation, yet good roads connect all major cities and most secondary towns.

# 1) The Land

The Republic of El Salvador, which has an area of 8,260 square miles, is the smallest country of Central America and the only one without a Caribbean coast. Slightly smaller than Massachusetts and roughly rectangular, El Salvador measures about 150 miles from west to east and 50 miles from north to south.

Much of El Salvador is mountainous, as are its bordering neighbors, Guatemala on the west and Honduras on the north and east. The Gulf of Fonseca also forms a portion of El Salvador's eastern boundary, separating the country from Nicaragua, while the Pacific Ocean establishes the southern Salvadoran border. El Salvador also owns several small islands offshore in the gulf, whose navigable waters it shares with Honduras and Nicaragua.

## Topography

El Salvador has three main topographical regions, each determined by altitude. The coastal lowlands, called the *tierra caliente* (torrid land), consist of a narrow, fertile plain that runs the length of the Pacific coast and extends 10 to 20 miles inland. Substantial areas of this region are used to raise cotton and sugarcane or to graze

The central highlands of rural El Salvador form a patchwork quilt of fields that are cultivated down to the edge of the road or property line. Farm families often live in villages to conserve precious land for agriculture.

Courtesy of Inter-American Development Bank

cattle, often on large commercial plantations called haciendas. The beaches along the coast are of volcanic origin and have black sand. There is little surf, though the beaches are pounded by heaving swells. Imposing volcanic cliffs and headlands rise out of the ocean and separate beaches from one another.

The central highlands, whose average elevation is 2,000 feet, support most of the country's farms, industries, and people. This area consists of a broad valley or plateau between two mountain ranges: the southern coastal range and the interior highlands in the north. The higher slopes in the central highlands are ideal for the cultivation of coffee. The land on the lower slopes is farmed intensively to feed a rapidly growing population. Salvadorans call the central highlands the *tierra templada* (land of the moderate climate).

Also with a temperate climate, but with a less hospitable topography, are the interior highlands, which are much more

Courtesy of David Mangurian

Located near the Pacific coast, Izalco Volcano looks peaceful and quiet today, but from 1770, when it first erupted, to 1966, it was constantly active. The eruptions provided men at sea with an easily seen beacon of fire to guide them on their journeys.

rugged and thinly populated. The land here is neither level nor even moderately hilly. Yet, wherever it is possible to cultivate the soil, a farm or small settlement will be tucked into the mountainous terrain.

## Volcanoes

Six volcanoes are located in the central highlands of El Salvador at regular intervals from west to east and add a dramatic accent to the landscape. One of them, Santa Ana, is the country's highest peak (7,800 feet) and overlooks the city of the same name. Volcanoes also overlook San Salvador (the capital) and the smaller cities of Cojutepeque, San Vicente, and San Miguel.

Much seismic activity, such as the devastating October 1986 earthquake in San Salvador that registered 7.5 on the Richter scale, has occurred in the volcanic zone. Volcanic activity of past centuries has endowed central El Salvador with rich soil. Travelers sometimes cross large, forbidding expanses of jagged, black basalt —the residue of past eruptions—on Salvadoran roads. The craters of long-extinct volcanoes have become clear, blue lakes.

Izalco Volcano, located less than 20 miles from the Pacific Ocean, was long known to sailors as the Lighthouse of the Pacific. It erupted continuously for nearly two centuries until 1966. The San Miguel Volcano (6,994 feet) erupted in 1986, and fresh volcanic activity remains a constant threat.

The Fifth of November Dam located on the Lempa River has helped to increase El Salvador's hydroelectric capacity from 50,800 kilowatts in 1956 to 244,000 kilowatts in the early 1980s.

Beautiful Lake Ilopango, just a half hour by car from the capital, is really the deep crater of an extinct volcano now filled with clear, blue water. A favorite vacation spot, the lake offers swimming and fishing to those who can afford leisure and recreation.

## Waterways

El Salvador's only important river is the Lempa, which rises in Guatemala. Its waters, brown with silt from the mountains through which they have passed, form part of the border with Honduras before they empty into the Pacific. Fertile bottomlands along the Lempa are farmed intensively, down to the river's edge. Some 150 tributaries and streams that feed into the river drain a large area of El Salvador. Hydroelectric turbines powered by the flow of the Lempa—such as those of the Fifth of November and Cerrón Grande dams—provide more than 60 percent of El Salvador's electricity. Two other rivers of much less importance, the La Paz River on the Guatemalan border and the San Miguel River in eastern El Salvador, drain smaller areas.

The country's four sizable lakes, all located in extinct volcanoes, are popular places to swim and fish. Lake Güija is on the Guatemalan border in the northwest, while Lake Olomega is in the east. Lake Coatepeque and Lake Ilopango are located respectively west and east of San Salvador.

Lake Coatepeque is another volcano that stopped erupting long ago whose gaping cone has filled with water.

In addition to calderas (crater-lakes), El Salvador has many small natural lakes. Lake Apastepeque is surrounded by fields cultivated down to the water's edge.

11

Courtesy of David Mangurian

From the air, the Salvadoran countryside looks as if it has been overlaid with mesh, creating small, neat squares, arched indentations, and soldier-straight lines of trees.

## Climate

El Salvador is located in the tropics, but its many elevations vary its climate. Most Salvadorans live in the central highlands, where the climate is healthy and invigorating and where the average annual temperature is about 73° F. In contrast, along the Pacific coast it is often oppressively hot, with temperatures averaging 10 degrees higher.

There are distinct wet and dry seasons. The rainy period, called the *invierno*, extends from May to October, with showers falling almost every afternoon. Annual rainfall amounts to 60 inches in the central and interior highlands and to 85 inches along the coast.

## Flora and Fauna

El Salvador was once heavily forested, but today woods cover only about 7 percent of the country and are mainly concentrated in the north and south—mountainous areas with few people. The trees here are deciduous, some common examples being dogwood, mahogany, walnut, rubber, and ceiba. Less rugged areas have grasslands and sparse forests of oak, cedar, and pine. Lowland regions of the country are conspicuous for their abundance of tropical fruits and medicinal plants.

Deer, pumas, jaguars, ocelots, peccaries —a variety of wild pig—coyotes, and tapirs (related to the horse and rhinoceros) are still found in the mountains, but increased population has led to the destruction of once-abundant animal life. In the lagoons of the hot, humid areas of the southern plain, there are armadillos, turtles, iguanas, caimans, and alligators, as well as many snakes, including the boa constrictor. This area is also home to the quetzal, a bright-plumed member of the trogon family of birds. Offshore, the Pacific waters abound with fish, including groupers, mullet, anchovies, tuna, and sea bass.

## Natural Resources

The country is poor in mineral resources. There are no known sources of petroleum, though El Salvador has a small refinery where imported oil is processed into gasoline and other petroleum derivatives. Gold and silver in small amounts have been found in the mountains of Morazán department in the northeast. El Salvador has substantial quantities of quartz, gypsum, limestone, and pumice and produces cement, lime, salt (extracted from the Pacific Ocean waters), gravel, and slate.

The country's hardwood trees—including mahogany and walnut—are sufficient to support a growing furniture industry. The light and buoyant wood of the balsa tree has long been used for raft and boat

The boa constrictor is found in both Central and South America and is so called because it kills by crushing the bones of its prey, rather than by venom, or poison. Adult boas reach an average length of 10 feet, although 14-foot specimens have been recorded.

13

Fish figure prominently among El Salvador's fauna and natural resources. Sharks are landed from Pacific waters for their valuable livers, from which a rich, nutritious oil is obtained.

Located at an elevation of approximately 2,000 feet, San Salvador enjoys a mild climate. Days are often hot, and nights are uniformly pleasant. The city suffers from pollution owing to its location within a valley surrounded by hills and to the lack of any controls on automotive emissions.

In downtown San Salvador, the streets are crowded to capacity during working days, and the press of people can be exhausting. Because Salvadorans like to lunch at home, rush hour occurs not twice but four times a day, creating a commuter bedlam of fumes and bumper-to-bumper traffic.

In contrast, during the long midday siesta or in the evening after the government and business workers have gone home, the heart of the city undergoes a welcome transformation. A casual feeling descends and there is leisure to admire the Renaissance-style National Palace, where the National Assembly meets, and the magnificently restored National Theater.

building. Another valuable tree is the *Myroxylon pereirae,* an evergreen that produces a sticky reddish-brown substance used in perfumes, confections, and medicines. Because of their commercial importance, this evergreen and the balsa are El Salvador's national trees.

## Cities

San Salvador (Holy Savior) is the capital and largest city of El Salvador and its commercial, cultural, and political center. Originally founded in 1525 some 25 miles north of its present site, colonial San Salvador was totally destroyed by an earthquake in 1854 and later rebuilt. The new modern city has few architectural reminders of its Spanish past. San Salvador proper has a population of 450,000, although the greater metropolitan area has over one million people—nearly one-fifth of El Salvador's total population.

In El Salvador's tropical climate, palm trees of many varieties thrive and often line the roads and avenues of large and small cities.

The houses of the well-to-do of San Salvador recall Old World architectural influences of both Spanish and Moorish origin. The white exteriors protect the residents from the heat, while the red-tiled roofs serve as picturesque ornamentation as well as a practical shield against the seasonal rains.

The ornate Basilica of San Salvador and the old post office buildings are also beautiful structures.

Beyond the downtown area lie some of the most pleasant suburbs in the Americas. Set at a higher altitude, above the hurly-burly of downtown, the city's suburbs have broad, tree-lined streets and ranch-style homes with fine lawns and gardens. The residences of San Salvador's middle and upper classes can be seen from the street, as in the United States. They are not hidden from view by the high protective walls so common in most Latin American cities.

Nine years of civil strife have swelled the size of slums in San Salvador and in secondary cities that are near the scenes of the most intense fighting. El Salvador's slums are places of extreme poverty and misery, reminders of the inequalities between rich and poor. In the west, sprawling ghettos and massive unemployment afflict Santa Ana, whose metropolitan population has grown to more than 200,000 in the past decade. Similarly, Sonsonate's population has increased from 31,000 in 1968 to more than 50,000; many of the city's residents side with the rebels. In the east, San Miguel's population

The sprawling old Central Market in downtown San Salvador is crowded with people buying and selling food under unsanitary conditions. Many such markets exist throughout El Salvador and often occupy several city blocks. In recent years, the government has begun to erect smaller public markets housed in buildings.

**15**

stands at more than 100,000; fully half of that figure reflects the influx of peasants fleeing the bloody fighting in the vicinity of their lands.

Not far from San Salvador, two other cities, Nueva San Salvador (called Santa Tecla) and Ciudad Delgado, have also grown quickly. In part, this has occurred because of the wartime boom in San Salvador's economy. People from Tecla and Delgado commute daily to the capital to avail themselves of the many new jobs.

Even during wartime, a somewhat more settled state of affairs has prevailed at ports on the Pacific, which are farther removed from hostilities. These cities include the popular seaside resort of Acajutla in the west, from which about 40 percent of El Salvador's coffee is exported, and La Unión in the southeast, the main port on the Gulf of Fonseca. With its flat terrain and good anchorages able to berth large oceangoing vessels, La Unión handles about half of all Salvadoran trade.

Olmec boulders are enormous stone heads that may be representations of Olmec rulers. The stones weigh as much as 40 tons and are 8 or 9 feet in height. The boulder that confirmed the presence of the Olmecs in El Salvador was found at Chalchuapa, in Santa Ana department.

# 2) History and Government

According to archaeologists, Indians migrated into the area of present-day El Salvador 3,000 years before the birth of Christ. There are various theories as to why they came; the most widely accepted view is that they were part of a general Asian migration across the Bering Strait and down the North American continent.

## The Olmecs

Among the earliest traceable inhabitants were the Olmecs, who may have been the earliest people of record in all of Middle America (as Mexico and Central America together are sometimes called). Olmec culture was centered near the present Mexican port of Veracruz, on the Gulf of Mexico, and flourished around 2000 B.C. One of the evidences of the tribe's migration to El Salvador is the so-called Olmec Boulder, which was found on a coffee plantation near Chalchuapa. The four sides of the stone are carved in low relief with images of fierce warriors, whose faces have the "jaguar look," a common motif of Olmec art.

## The Lencas

A people known as the Lencas also inhabited El Salvador at one time, perhaps as long ago as 300 B.C. The Lencas had their main base at Usulután, in eastern El

Salvador, from which they traveled widely, trading their distinctive and high-quality pottery. The Lencas seem to have been influenced by several Indian cultures, including those of the Maya and of tribes to the southeast—in Nicaragua, Costa Rica, and perhaps the South American mainland. Some authorities even suspect Incan influence.

## Teotihuacán and Toltec Influences

Before A.D. 500, perhaps centuries earlier, Aztecs from Teotihuacán, just north of Mexico City, reached El Salvador. Their influence is reflected in ruins near the present city of Ahuachapán. After the fall of Teotihuacán in about A.D. 650, the Aztec temples in El Salvador were destroyed and their sculptures and monuments were broken, defaced, and buried—evidence that Teotihuacán power came to an abrupt and total end. After that time, the Toltecs, another people whose culture stemmed from further north of Mexico City, came to El Salvador, but they too eventually passed from the scene.

## The Maya

The Maya, a remarkable, highly cultured people whose cities stretched from southern Mexico to Honduras, also settled in El Salvador, mainly west of the Lempa River. The imposing temple ruins and ceremonial plazas found at Tazumal, Cihuatán, San Andrés, and Quelepa testify to their skill as architects and engineers.

Though it is uncertain when the Maya were El Salvador's most important inhabitants, their language was the principal one in use 1,500 years ago, and their system of religious worship was followed in most places at that time. They prayed to the sun and moon and appeased such other important deities as the rain god and corn god. Mayan merchants were important, widely traveled people protected by their own special gods. In addition to trading goods,

the merchants exchanged information and ideas and appear to have journeyed to the South American mainland, to many of the islands of the Caribbean, throughout Mexico, and quite likely to Florida.

A Mayan jar decorated with sculptured heads and other ornamentation, including glyphs, may be 1,500 years old.

Independent Picture Service

There are Mayan ruins throughout El Salvador, although most are west of the Lempa River. These pyramidal remains at Tazumal near Chalchuapa have been partly restored by archaeologists.

Courtesy of United Nations

Many of the Mayan ruins at San Andrés in western El Salvador have yet to be excavated. The significance and history of the mound (*upper left*), for example, are still unknown.

**19**

The Aztec calendar, said to be based on an earlier Mayan system, was used by the lesser-advanced Pipil Indians to regulate times of planting and harvesting. Calendars employed glyphs or carved images such as are on the Stone of the Sun (*left*). The calendar system consisted of 365 days, which were divided into 18 months of 20 days each. There were 5 additional "hollow" days that were regarded as ill omened.

## The Pipils

When the Spaniards arrived in the sixteenth century, the Pipils—a nomadic tribe that spoke the Nahua tongue of Mexico's Indians—were dominant in El Salvador. Over the course of earlier centuries, the Pipils spread, or were driven, south and east from southern Mexico through Guatemala and eventually occupied almost all of El Salvador and neighboring areas of modern-day Honduras and Nicaragua.

The Pipil Indians reached El Salvador in the eleventh century A.D. and for four centuries lived a settled, agricultural existence. Culturally, they were not as advanced as the Maya, from whom they borrowed many traits, but they were tough, warlike, and usually victorious. Their ancient capital, Cuscatlán (city of riches), was near the present town of Cihuatán, where there are extensive ruins. Traces of the once-powerful Pipils are found throughout El Salvador.

Like other inhabitants of Central America, the Pipils cultivated maize as their main food crop. They worshipped corn and rain gods and carried out religious cere-

Pedro de Alvarado was a senior officer in the Spanish forces sent to the New World to explore and colonize. Second in command to Hernando Cortés in their conquest of Mexico, Alvarado himself was the conqueror of the present-day nations of El Salvador and Guatemala. He was killed in 1541 during an Indian rebellion in Mexico.

monies similar to those of the Maya and the Aztecs. They regulated their lives—the times of planting, harvesting, and major ceremonies—using the remarkably accurate Mayan or Aztec calendar. The Pipils were skilled in architecture, astronomy, and crafts such as weaving, pottery, stone carving, and the working of gold and silver. They could make complicated mathematical computations by using a number system that was based on units of 20, not 10 (as is our own) and included the concept of zero—something unknown to the ancient Greeks and Romans.

## The Spanish Conquest

The relatively advanced Pipil civilization attracted the interest and greed of Spanish explorers and conquistadors. In 1528, the Pipils succumbed to Don Pedro de Alvarado—a lieutenant of Hernando Cortés, the captain general of New Spain—but only after putting up a stubborn fight for three years. In their first battle, the Pipils actually defeated the Spaniards and severely wounded Alvarado. This was one of the few major defeats suffered by the conquistadors anywhere in the Western Hemisphere.

Once subdued, the Pipils settled down and in a fairly short time adapted themselves to the culture and religion of the invading Spaniards. Induced to work for the Spanish colonists, the Pipils built colonial towns and churches and added their own unmistakable motifs to the ornamentation.

Before long the bloodlines of the conquerors and the conquered were blended in children of mixed parentage. Those who adopted the Spanish rather than the In-dian way of living were called Ladinos, and most people in the country had become Ladinos by 1700. But the process was not always peaceful. Intermittently during the colonial period, and even later, the Pipil Indians rebelled, only to be put down with bloody reprisals. During a rebellion in 1932, as many as 30,000 Indians were slaughtered in the name of peace and public order in the southwest department of Sonsonate.

## Spanish Rule

From 1525 until 1821, the territory and people of what became El Salvador were governed as part of Spain's empire in the Western Hemisphere. Whatever governing arrangements the Indians had had were overturned and destroyed. El Salva-

Courtesy of Earl H. Lubensky

**Part of the Spanish approach to colonization of new areas was to build—and not only on the grand scale. Simple village churches were erected throughout the newly conquered land and are today vivid reminders of El Salvador's Spanish colonial roots.**

22

The first city of San Salvador was not the only casualty of El Salvador's earthquake-prone land. The ruins of a village church located near Izalco testify to the destructive power of seismic activity.

dor, a province of New Spain—as Mexico was then called—was under the immediate jurisdiction and rule of a royal official called a captain general whose headquarters were in Guatemala City.

The first city called San Salvador was founded in 1525, near the former Pipil capital, Cuscatlán. In 1526, however, the city was destroyed by an earthquake. In 1528 a second effort at settlement was made, but the city, which was established in the Valley of La Bermuda, failed to prosper. In 1545 San Salvador was permanently founded in the Valley of the Hamacas, its present location.

During centuries of colonial rule, El Salvador was a sort of no-man's-land between Guatemala and Nicaragua. Few settlers were interested in developing land where valuable mineral resources were scarce and where there was little cheap labor to exploit them. The Spanish crown paid scant attention to the small province that repaid royal efforts with little revenue—crown officials did not often invest funds in unprofitable colonial enterprises. Sleepy and backward, El Salvador was considered one of the least important parts of the vast Spanish Empire and remained neglected for 250 years.

Things took a turn for the better only in the latter part of the eighteenth century. Cattle raising and the production of indigo—a deep blue dye used to color cotton and wool—became profitable and widespread. Consequently, the population increased and San Salvador came to be the second most important city in the captaincy general, after Guatemala City. In 1786 this changed situation was officially recognized when El Salvador's status was raised to that of an intendency—a Spanish colonial ranking that gave the province more authority over its local affairs and equal administrative standing with Nicaragua and Honduras.

The successful U.S. and French revolutions of the late eighteenth century brought new ideas that helped to undermine the rigid stability of both the Church and the royal government in El Salvador. The notions of liberty, democracy, and the value of human reason—as opposed to divinely revealed truth—became widespread and popular, even in a place as remote as El Salvador. These ideas, plus the unwelcome interference in Spanish affairs by Napoleon Bonaparte, who forcibly placed his brother Joseph on the Spanish throne, awakened Salvadoran yearnings for freedom.

The first serious challenges to Spanish rule in Central America took place in El Salvador. In 1811, a local priest, José Matías Delgado, started a revolt to gain independence. While this action was sternly put down, it stimulated similar uprisings in Guatemala and Nicaragua. Three years later, a local leader, Manuel José Arce, started another revolt, which was also suppressed.

## Struggle for Independence

When independence finally came to El Salvador, it was as part of an action taken together by all the Central American provinces. In 1821, Mexico won its independence under the leadership of Agustín de Iturbide, who, after assuming the title of Emperor Agustín I, invited the Central American provinces to become annexed to his empire. All agreed except El Salvador, and Mexican troops poured into the unyielding country to satisfy Iturbide's imperial ambitions. Though the troops occupied the country, they could not break the people's will. At one point, the Salvadorans appealed to the United States to grant their country statehood, as a way of protecting it from Iturbide. Fortunately, the problem lasted only a short time. In 1823, Iturbide was overthrown and shot, and El Salvador was free to follow its own destiny.

In that same year, El Salvador became part of the Federation of Central America, with its capital at Guatemala City and Manuel José Arce as its first president. From the outset, factional strife doomed this experiment in regional government, as Liberals fought against Conservatives, pro-Church people opposed anticlericals,

Independent Picture Service

Francisco Morazán, a Honduran, was president of the Federation of Central America to which El Salvador belonged between 1830 and 1839.

and those who wanted home rule battled those who wanted to centralize governing power in Guatemala.

By 1827, the federation was wracked by civil war. Guerrilla bands representing various political positions terrorized many parts of the country. In 1829, the Honduran leader, Francisco Morazán, occupied Guatemala City and took over the presidency. In 1835, he moved the capital of the federation to San Salvador.

In 1838, Rafael Carrera, an illiterate Guatemalan peasant, spearheaded a Conservative-backed revolt. By 1840, he had led his mobs of fanatical supporters to victory and to the creation of a separate, independent Guatemala. The Federation of Central America ended. El Salvador began its life as a solely independent republic in 1838, as a result of Carrera's Guatemalan revolution.

## Nationhood

El Salvador's first "independent" government was imposed on the country by the victorious Carrera and was strongly conservative in tone. It tolerated no interference with the dominance of the upper class or with the established position of the Church in national life. For the next two decades, liberal and conservative governments alternated in power—often drawing on meddlesome foreign interests for support. As a rule, Liberals favored decentralized governments and a reduction in the influence of the Church. Conservatives looked to the Church as a pillar of support and backed strong central governments that were responsive to the landed aristocracy.

A long series of short-term presidents followed—five of whom were overthrown by revolution and two of whom were assassinated—before the country experienced its first real dictators, Santiago González, who held power from 1871 to 1875, and Carlos Ezeta, who was in office from 1890 to 1894. While the record of El Salvador's experience with self-government under democratic forms hardly appears a happy one, it was scarcely a deviation from the norm of other Latin American countries at this time. During the first three decades of the twentieth century, El Salvador achieved a form of political stability, with a few ruling families (stereotyped as *Los Catorce Grandes,* or "the 14 Families") monopolizing power to support and further their own interests. Under these conditions, the transfer of political power was accomplished peacefully at regular intervals, as one member of the ruling oligarchy succeeded another.

But in 1931, at a time of depressed coffee prices, General Maximiliano Hernández Martínez seized dictatorial power, retaining it until a revolution by students and soldiers overthrew him in 1944. Hernández's coup represented the first purely military takeover in the country's history. Although democratic practices were weakened by his rule, some material advantages, mainly benefiting the well-to-do, were introduced to the country.

Following Hernández's overthrow, El Salvador adopted a new constitution in

**Material advantages, such as improved farming and transportation methods, generally never affected the mass of Salvadorans in the nineteenth century. For centuries, ox-driven carts brought goods into the villages, just as they still do today.**

Funds from international organizations such as the World Bank gave El Salvador the means to build hydroelectric dams, which now provide 60 percent of all the electricity used in the nation.

1950 that lasted for 12 years. Under it, El Salvador enjoyed considerable economic progress, including the building of dams and power plants on the Lempa River and the renewal of regional interest in a Central American common market. Successive governments, though relying on the nation's oligarchy and military for support, made efforts to solve social problems in areas such as housing, education, and health conditions.

## Alliances

In the 1960s, El Salvador became a leader in promoting the Alliance for Progress, a program through which the United States and Latin American countries sought to accelerate development of the Western Hemisphere's nations and to enhance the lives of their people. With U.S. foreign aid and loans from the newly created Inter-American Development Bank, the Salvadoran government—despite limited

With the help of foreign funds, Salvadoran governments of the 1950s continued to build sections of the Pan-American Highway. This stretch of road is kilometer 46 as it looked in March of 1950.

amounts of financial siphoning for personal use—undertook crash projects to meet the social needs of its people and to create new industries and sources of wealth.

The spirit of cooperation with neighboring nations seemed to take deep root in El Salvador. The country became a leader in the formation of the Central American Common Market (CACM), a historic move whereby the five signatories (the other four were Guatemala, Honduras, Nicaragua, and Costa Rica) contracted to open their markets to one another. El Salvador was quick to expand its manufacturing capabilities to produce goods for the regional market.

Unfortunately, however, not even the CACM was enough to offset El Salvador's need for new jobs to cope with its rapidly growing population. Over the course of several decades, some 300,000 Salvadorans, unable to find work or farmland

The reactivated interest in the Central American Common Market eventually provided El Salvador's craftspersons with an outlet for their goods.

A 12-year-old boy in the village of Ilobasco paints original Mayan designs on clay plates before they are fired a second time. This type of pottery is both sold within El Salvador and exported to regional and international markets.

in their own country, immigrated to Honduran territory, often crossing the poorly guarded mountain borders illegally, without the necessary papers.

## War with Honduras

In early 1969, the Honduran government, experiencing its own domestic problems, began to speak out on the Salvadoran "invasion" of Honduran territory. In the Honduran border towns, Salvadoran currency circulated freely and Salvadoran émigrés developed important businesses. Hondurans saw the Salvadorans as an economic threat.

Numerous incidents occurred, mainly cases in which Hondurans beat or robbed Salvadoran emigrants. Reports of these incidents, greatly magnified in the Salvadoran press, roused much public feeling in El Salvador. The matter became a crisis when Honduras passed land legislation

Independent Picture Service

During the 100-hour-long Soccer War, young Salvadoran soldiers raise their arms in celebration of victory after taking Nueva Ocotepeque, a small provincial city that serves as the capital of Ocotepeque department. Nueva Ocotepeque lies just inside the southwestern border of Honduras, roughly 10 miles from Salvadoran territory.

Independent Picture Service

The hills of El Amatillo provided Salvadoran artillery with enough cover to surprise and destroy a convoy of Honduran trucks in the opening hours of the 1969 war. Of the hundreds of civilians and soldiers killed and wounded, most were Honduran. It was estimated that 50,000 people from both countries lost their homes or had their fields—and thus their livelihoods—destroyed or damaged during the conflict. The cost of the devastation was roughly assessed at $50 million.

The citizens of the capital city of San Salvador welcome home their soldiers after the short-but-bloody Soccer War.

that would dispossess even second- or third-generation Salvadorans if their ancestors had settled in Honduras without the necessary legal documentation.

To protect the interests of their fellow citizens, Salvadoran troops invaded Honduras in July 1969. The ensuing conflict lasted 100 hours and left 1,000 dead and 4,000 wounded. It came to be known as the "Soccer War," because actual shooting was preceded by a series of hotly contested soccer games between the two countries. The causes of the conflict, however, were rooted in animosities, such as national prejudice and hunger for land, that were as old as Central America itself. A cease-fire was arranged under the guidance of the Organization of American States, and a peace treaty with Honduras was formally signed in 1980.

In addition to the numbers of dead and wounded caused by 1969 hostilities between El Salvador and Honduras, each side took prisoners of war. Salvadoran soldiers return to their country in a two-way exchange arranged by the International Red Cross.

29

For El Salvador, the cost of its brief war with Honduras was high, since it precipitated the breakdown of the CACM. After the war, Honduras closed off its roads to Salvadoran commerce, thus cutting off El Salvador from trade by land with three of its common market partners, Nicaragua, Costa Rica, and Honduras itself.

During the 1970s, El Salvador's economy languished. Foreign business firms, attracted to the country during the CACM boom, invested job-creating resources elsewhere. Salvadorans of means, alarmed by the unsettled conditions at home, reinvested their capital abroad, mainly in the safe haven of the United States.

Successive governments, dominated by the military, proved unable to halt these trends. Spokesmen in opposition to the government, including priests who openly championed the rights of the nation's poor, drew large crowds. The brutal murder of Archbishop Oscar Arnulfo Romero y Galdames in 1980 ignited a wave of violence. By dawn of the day following the assassination, 30 bombs had exploded, damaging banks and businesses. During the homily for the slain prelate at the Metropolitan Cathedral of San Salvador, repeated gunfire and explosions created panic among the 75,000 mourners and left 30 dead, hundreds wounded.

Photo by Charles Borniger

**Prolonged hostilities affect many aspects of ordinary life in El Salvador. Mass is celebrated to honor civilians killed in a rural skirmish, as government forces stand guard. Innocent bystanders are often victims in a conflict that has no fixed front lines and in which bloodshed occurs wherever rebel and government troops encounter each other.**

## Civil War

The stage was set for the establishment of a lasting insurrectionary movement and for a civil war, which is still in progress. One of the conflict's principal actors is José Napoleón Duarte, a graduate of the University of Notre Dame, who was appointed president of El Salvador by a ruling junta in December of 1980. Duarte was elected president in his own right in 1984, following a transitional coalition government and the writing of a new constitution by an elected constituent assembly.

From the outset of Duarte's political rule, he has counted on staunch support from the U.S. administration of President Ronald Reagan. Shortly after Reagan's inauguration in 1981, the United States began supplying El Salvador with large-scale financial and military assistance. U.S. military advisors have helped train

Photo by Charles Borniger

President Duarte, El Salvador's chief executive, affectionately greets the mother of one of his bodyguards—a captain killed by rebel terrorists.

Photo by Charles Borniger

During the Reagan administration, which began in 1981, U.S.-supplied helicopters have become more common in El Salvador.

31

Among the targets of rebel attacks in 1984 was the newly constructed San Lorenzo hydroelectric dam. Soldiers of the National Guard defend San Ildefonzo airstrip, which brings men and material to the site. Such airstrips are also used by U.S. military advisors. The airstrip at Ilopango was the departure point for the U.S.-financed plane that was shot down by the Nicaraguans in October 1986. The downed aircraft was on a contra supply mission to southern Nicaragua.

Courtesy of Inter-American Development Bank

Salvadoran government forces to fight the insurgents and are stationed at the headquarters of battalion units fighting in the field.

In return for its assistance, the United States has insisted that the Salvadoran government make progress in curbing violations of human rights and in eliminating the use of assassination to quell political dissent. The U.S. administration has also insisted that the Salvadoran government attack the roots of public discontent and mount an effective land reform program. The Reagan administration believes that the main rebel forces—under the banner of the Farabundo Martí National Liberation Front (FMLN)—are dedicated Communists and depend for supplies and advice on Cuba, Nicaragua, and other socialist governments.

Hopes for a peaceful settlement were raised in 1984 when Duarte met with rebel leaders in the village of La Palma to discuss ways to achieve an end to the conflict. Following the meeting in La Palma, the fighting intensified and then seemed to wane. In October 1985, however, the rebels staged a daring raid on the main government training camp during which more than 40 government soldiers were killed. Since then, the level of field combat has diminished, but the fighting has taken a nasty turn involving urban terrorism and the killing of innocent civilians.

## Guatemala Accord

In February 1987 Costa Rican president Oscar Arias Sánchez put forth a Central American peace proposal. Arias' plan—since referred to as the Guatemala Accord—called for scheduled cease-fires, free elections, committees to solve local disagreements, and other democratic re-

In October of 1984, government officials and rebels in arms – the latter headed by Guillermo Ungo, president of the Democratic Revolutionary Front of the Farabundo Martí National Liberation Front (FMLN) – met face-to-face for over four hours in the village of La Palma. The meeting, arranged by Roman Catholic prelates, failed to achieve a cease-fire but stimulated hopes of an eventual negotiated settlement of the conflict. Ironically, Ungo was once the vice presidential running mate of his counterpart at the negotiating table – President Duarte. Further talks were arranged by the Church in the villages of Ayagualo in 1984 and Sesori in 1986 (the Sesori talks were postponed). Duarte is anxious to integrate the guerrillas into the political process and has offered amnesty to FMLN members, but only if they first lay down their arms. The rebels want to be part of a provisional government that would arrange new elections, and they also demand that their fighters become part of the Salvadoran armed forces. So far, Duarte has rejected both ideas as unconstitutional.

Photo by Charles Borniger

forms. On August 7, 1987, the chief executives of Honduras, El Salvador, Nicaragua, Guatemala, and Costa Rica met to sign the accord.

By early 1988 only Costa Rica had abided by all the provisions of the peace accord. Both El Salvador and Nicaragua have complied, however, with at least some of the peace plan initiatives.

In El Salvador, the government allowed civilians who openly support the rebel cause to return to the capital city of San Salvador. The Salvadoran government also released several hundred prisoners who were suspected of being members of the rebel army. In granting amnesty to these political prisoners, however, the government also overturned sentences, which included the murder of civilians, against members of its own army.

Nicaragua freed almost 1,000 political prisoners and agreed to participate in peace talks with the contra rebels. Moreover, the government has permitted the operation of an anti-government newspaper and radio station. In contrast to this, however, Nicaraguan officials plan to boost the country's army reserve to half a million troops—a move that would contradict the goals of the peace accord.

## Government

El Salvador is a democratic republic operating under a new constitution ratified in December 1983. This document, superseding the previous constitution of 1962, provides for a three-part governmental system, consisting of executive, legislative, and judicial branches.

Executive power is vested in a president, who is elected for a five-year term and is ineligible for immediate reelection. A 60-member, single-chamber legislative body, called the National Assembly, comprises representatives elected by popular vote for two-year terms. Judicial authority is exercised by an independent Supreme Court.

For administrative purposes, the country is divided into 14 departments, each headed by a governor appointed by the central government to a four-year term. In turn, the departments are separated into districts called *municipios* (municipalities).

Early in 1988 President Duarte faced one of his most difficult challenges. The right-wing National Republic Alliance (ARENA) upset the president's majority representation in El Salvador's National Assembly. Duarte's control over his own party has weakened, and the Christian Democrats face stiff competition in the next presidential election from ARENA's probable choice of a candidate, Alfredo Cristiani. Should Cristiani—a politically moderate ARENA member—become El Salvador's new president, the U.S. Congress may reduce its economic aid to the nation.

Courtesy of Earl H. Lubensky

The variety of underground political groups in El Salvador is wide. The BPR—Bloque Popular Revolucionario—used a tempting white wall to profess one of its political credos: "Defend the right to a job and life." The FMLN itself acts as a political-military umbrella for at least five revolutionary organizations.

The neoclassical-style City Hall stands in the city of Santa Ana, which is located approximately 37 miles from the capital city of San Salvador.

Crowded, outdoor marketplaces reflect the urban population problems faced by El Salvador, as entire rural families move to already thronging cities in an effort to escape civil strife.

# 3) The People

With nearly 700 people per square mile, El Salvador, population 5.3 million, is the most densely populated and one of the fastest-growing nations on the American mainland. At 2.6 percent, its present rate of annual increase, El Salvador's population will double within 27 years.

Where and how all the new people will live are questions that deeply preoccupy Salvadorans. At the moment, the press of people is most acutely felt in the central highlands, where the Salvadoran popula-

tion has been concentrated for centuries. The civil strife of recent years has intensified population pressures in this area, as farm families have sought refuge in the growing cities from the rural fighting. This movement of people from rural to urban areas has led to the creation of large metropolitan slums, filled with unskilled people who have overloaded El Salvador's already inadequate social welfare system.

Yet, despite this migration of people, three of five Salvadorans continue to live on farms or in villages. As might be expected, the worst living conditions prevail in areas of the most civil unrest. These include mountainous areas along the Honduran border, where nearly two-thirds of the people are without pure drinking water and where open sewers serve as breeding grounds for disease.

For centuries, the people of rural El Salvador have borne deprivation with patience. But lately, with the availability of inexpensive transistor radios and with other improvements in communications, rural Salvadorans have become aware of their social and economic neglect. They have come to understand that they receive little attention from the central government in San Salvador. This awareness makes them sympathetic to calls for revolution from rebels who live among them and who share their daily misery.

## Ethnic Origins

Racial mixing over many centuries has created a Salvadoran population that is about 92 percent mestizo. Five percent are white, and the remaining 3 percent are pure Indian. Salvadorans are proud of their Indian heritage. Appeals to patriotism often depict the brave and warlike

Courtesy of Earl H. Lubensky

In rural areas, where the only fuel is firewood or charcoal, meals are of necessity prepared in the old-fashioned way— outdoors on stone ovens.

Courtesy of Earl H. Lubensky

Near Cihuatán, Candelario Ramirez drinks water from a *tecomate*, or gourd—a typical means of carrying safe water in remote areas where pure drinking water is hard to find.

Pipil Indians who resisted the Spanish conquerors to the death. Even Salvadorans classified as white identify with their country's Indian forebears.

El Salvador's few surviving Indians live mostly in the southwestern highlands along the Guatemalan border. Some still speak the ancient Nahua language and cling to ancestral ways, even though they are surrounded by modern culture.

El Salvador's mestizos are serious, hardworking, and less given to the very open expressions of sorrow or joy shown by many other Central American peoples. Family ties among mestizos are strong. Often two or three generations of a family live under the same red-tiled roof. Families grow still larger when they bring in business associates or friends as godparents of children. Such extended families are often the networks through which businesses are operated, as well as the groups with whom sad or festive occasions are shared.

Successful mestizos consider themselves self-made. Those who have attained upper- or upper-middle-class standing often resent whites who have inherited wealth, a business, or a farm. Mestizos invest heavily in their children's education to prepare them for useful roles in society. They look forward to the day when merit, and not social position or wealth, will be the sole determinant of success in El Salvador.

Until the recent civil war, the mestizo middle class of El Salvador was rapidly expanding, partly as a result of the country's success in developing its industrial base. During the course of the war, this middle class has favored moderation: an end to the killing on both sides and the restoration of conditions essential to peaceful social and economic progress.

El Salvador's small, though still-powerful, white minority is centered in the capital city of San Salvador. Some of the country's prominent families trace their

Courtesy of Inter-American Development Bank

Higher education is taken seriously by successful mestizos, who view it as a means of circumventing the elitist social structure still in operation in the capital.

In the capital, many women work outside the home to make ends meet. The San Jacinto Market day-care center offers mothers a place to leave their children while they operate market stalls. For roughly 10 cents a day, each child is assured reliable supervision and a nutritious lunch.

lineage to the Spanish conquerors. Well-educated and well-traveled, San Salvador's ruling elite is cosmopolitan in taste and outlook and socially accomplished.

Women of this privileged group are in quiet revolt against the country's male-dominated society. They have taken leadership roles in promoting family planning to attack their country's population problem. Men, however, are still unquestionably preeminent at all levels. For many Salvadoran women, one of the appealing features of the rebellion is the prominence the movement accords to women in the ongoing insurrection.

## Education

El Salvador's poor record in public education is reflected in the fact that the country had no public education system at all until the middle of the nineteenth century. Lack of adequate schooling has been a primary cause of discontent. Even today,

With half of the population under the age of 18, children are everywhere in El Salvador. Inadequate provision for primary schooling will mean that a large proportion of the next generation will be illiterate.

Courtesy of David Mangurian

Courtesy of Inter-American Development Bank

A crowded lecture hall of students taking a required math course at José Simeón Cañas Central American University, shows the eagerness with which young Salvadorans approach education. Yet, places in institutions of higher learning are still not available to all those who desire them.

A schoolhouse leveled by a land mine intended for government troops is a typical incident in a conflict that flares up sporadically. Among many reasons for poor educational facilities in El Salvador is the damage done to school buildings by troops fighting in the ongoing civil war.

only 40 percent of those in rural areas and only 62 percent in urban areas are functionally literate. Since 46 percent of the country's population is under 15 years of age, this means a substantial portion of El Salvador's next generation will be unable to read and write.

The government has attacked the education problem in fits and starts. There were crash programs to construct schools in the 1960s. With financial assistance from the United States, the Salvadoran government rushed to completion an educational television network in the early 1970s. In what the government hoped would be a technological shortcut to uni-

versal literacy, powerful transmitters located at San Andrés, not far from San Salvador, broadcast basic education courses to an expanded number of classrooms. The transmitters represented a short-term solution to El Salvador's dire lack of qualified teachers.

But such efforts proved unequal to the challenge, and they were soon to be disrupted by civil strife. In 1960, El Salvador boasted that it had succeeded in placing 80 percent of its primary school-aged children in classrooms. Because of this early intensive effort, there was an increase in student enrollment at secondary and university levels in the 1980s,

**41**

In the 1970s, the main reading room of the Central Library of the University of El Salvador showed an obvious mixture of male and female students. Both professors and students at the university actively voice their views on political issues. Some damage was inflicted on the library holdings in the 1980 clash with government troops, and various academic disciplines have since suffered from a lack of proper research materials.

Courtesy of Inter-American Development Bank

although the figure for attendance of primary school-aged children plummeted to 61 percent during the same period.

The slowness in creating educational opportunities through the secondary level was matched in higher education. The University of El Salvador—the first in the country—was not founded until 1841. For many years its curriculum comprised just three courses—grammar, philosophy, and morals—and its first rector did double duty, directing the university as well as an exclusive secondary school whose facilities the university shared.

Today, the University of El Salvador accommodates 12,000 students with a full range of courses in several fields. Its student body is a lightning rod for opposition to the government. In July of 1980, government troops stormed the university,

citing it as a major source of subversive activity and political opposition. Several students were killed, and later that same year the university's rector was assassinated. The university is now officially open, but classes are interrupted frequently by both students and faculty members. Nevertheless, they have embarked upon more constructive activities, such as seeking educational funding and lobbying for broader academic opportunities. Consequently, the government has become less hostile and has respected more of the university's traditional autonomy.

Partly to provide an alternative to the increased politicization of the national university, a private Catholic institution, the José Simeón Cañas Central American University, was founded in 1965. It now has more than 6,000 students, many of them concentrating in business and engineering studies. Still another private institution, José Matías Delgado University, opened its doors in 1977 and now has nearly 4,000 students, many of them preparing for careers in public administration, business, and law.

But even with the new universities, the demand for higher education much exceeds available space. Families of means commonly send their children abroad, to universities and colleges in the United States and Western Europe. The situation is not much changed from Spanish colonial days when well-to-do parents sent their children to Spain, Mexico, or Guatemala to be educated.

## Health

Years of civil conflict have put an unusual strain on the government's endeavor to provide adequate health care for Salvadorans. Nevertheless, a number of public health schemes established before the war began still operate in both rural and urban areas. In addition, new programs are in place to modernize hospitals and to improve educational facilities for student nurses.

El Salvador's fast-growing population still outpaces the government's efforts to improve community health. By the late 1980s, the country's water and sewage systems provided only about 40 percent of rural dwellers and 67 percent of those living in urban areas with access to safe

Courtesy of Inter-American Development Bank

Students stroll on the campus of José Simeón Cañas Central American University, named to honor the priest who introduced a measure in 1823 to abolish slavery while serving as a member of the constitutent assembly of the Federation of Central America.

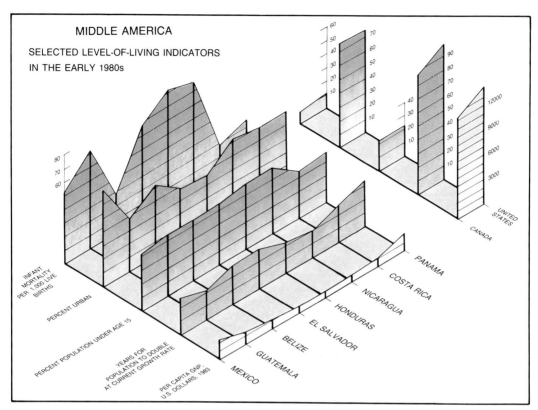

MIDDLE AMERICA

SELECTED LEVEL-OF-LIVING INDICATORS
IN THE EARLY 1980s

This graph shows how each of five factors, which are suggestive of the quality and style of life, varies among the eight Middle American countries. Canada and the United States are included for comparison. Data from "1986 World Population Data Sheet" (Washington, D.C.: Population Reference Bureau, Inc., 1986).

water. Between 1980 and 1985, a little over half of the nation's one-year-old children were immunized against diphtheria and measles. More successful programs either eliminated or greatly decreased the threat against the population of diseases such as yellow fever and malaria.

By 1987 El Salvador's infant mortality rate had dropped to 65 deaths out of every 1,000 live births. Although this figure represents an improvement for the country, it is well above the rate for industrialized nations. Salvadorans' life expectancy— about 66 years—ranks fourth among the Central American nations.

## Literature

Though small in size, El Salvador has produced many writers of note since its

independence in 1821. José Batres y Montúfar (1809–1844), the country's first nineteenth-century writer of distinction, wrote of the pattern of life during the late colonial period. He was followed closely by the poet Enrique Hoyos (1810–1859) and by later romantics, such as Ana Dolores Arias (1810–1859) and Rafael Cabrera (1860–1885). The most famous of the romantic-era poets, however, was José Cañas Gavidia (1826–1918), who spent much of his long life abroad and who wrote nostalgically of the lakes and volcanoes of his homeland.

Probably the giant of Salvadoran literature was Francisco Gavidia (1863–1955). A poet, philologist, translator, essayist, historian, and dramatist, he was the most important Salvadoran writer and intellectual of the first half of the twentieth

Volcanoes provided José Cañas Gavidia with ongoing inspiration for his poetry.

Courtesy of Earl H. Lubensky
Children are given the shells of turtles to play as ready-made drums—a popular Salvadoran instrument.

Independent Picture Service
Church music has been the most active area of orchestral and choral composition in El Salvador.

century. Gavidia worked ceaselessly to promote the establishment of a national theater, a dream still to be adequately realized. His most important poem was "To Central America," in which he condemned tyranny and expressed faith in the unity of the Central American countries. His *Princess Cavek* is a historical drama about pre-Spanish times; *The Book of Orange Blossoms* is a volume of poetry addressed to a young bride; and *A Modern History of El Salvador* deals mainly with the independence period. Gavidia's virtuoso display of talents continues to be a source of pride to the people of El Salvador.

Arturo Ambrogí (1875–1936) introduced popular prose to his people and was a disciple of Nicaragua's great Rubén Darío. Other, more recent writers of this century include the poets Carmen Brannon de Samayoa Chinchilla (pseudonym Claudia Lars; born 1899), Alberto Guerra Trigueros (1898–1950), and Hugo Lindo (born 1917). The best-known and most important contemporary literary figure is Salvador Salazar Arrué (born 1899), who signs his novels, short stories, and paintings with the pseudonym Salarrué. He has taken a conspicuous role in making the short story a prominent art form in Central America.

Among playwrights, J. Emilio Aragón (1887–1938) is best known for his political satires, while Walter Béneke's play *The Imprudents' Paradise* has found receptive audiences in Spain and Venezuela, as well as in Central America. Other modern dramatists of note are Waldo Chávez Velasco, a writer of fantasies, and Italo López Vallecillos and Alvaro Menén Desleal, popular authors of political and philosophical works of distinction.

## Music

Long before the Spanish conquest, music played an important part in Salvadoran life. Archaeologists have found various

**45**

kinds of musical instruments—whistles with several tones; pipes having as many as six finger holes; and drums of wood or clay called *huehuetls,* originally covered with deerskin. The marimba, a wooden xylophone, also has a long history and is still played today.

During the colonial period, primitive church music enjoyed a vogue. In 1845, however, José Escolástico Andrino organized a music school and 15 years later began the first symphonic orchestra. He also became the country's first composer —of church music, symphonies, and one opera.

By 1864 the Academy of Fine Arts had its own music school, and 10 years later the National Conservatory of Music was founded. A second symphony was organized in 1875, followed by others in two of the provinces. In 1883 a periodical devoted to music commenced publication.

A stone bust by José Mejía Vides, entitled *Cabeza Numero 1,* was awarded first prize in an arts competition.

*Cansancio* (Weariness) is the title of a work by Enrique Salaverria. The rough-hewn texture and simple lines of the stone suggest the fatigue of the burdened figures, perhaps depicting a mother and child.

Salvadoran composers have been numerous. Compositions by David Granadino and Felipe Soto, dating from the late nineteenth century, are still played. The twentieth-century composers Wenceslao García and María Mendoza de Baratta have both emphasized Indian themes.

El Salvador's fine National Symphony Orchestra is supported by both government and private sources. Under the baton of distinguished directors, the orchestra is a credit to the cultural life of the country.

## Painting

Painting has received less attention than music. No works of great significance were produced until a national school of painting developed in the late nineteenth and early twentieth centuries. Notable among the painters of this school were Juan Francisco Cisneros and Miguel Ortíz Villacorta.

Best known among present-day painters is José Mejía Vides (born 1923), who has

Among popular native crafts in El Salvador are baskets made of home-grown fibers, hand-carved figurines, and pottery jars.

been influenced by Mexico's famous muralists and who also reflects the French influence of Paul Gauguin. In direct and simple style, Mejía Vides depicts the villages of his home country. Other painters of the present day include Raul Elias Reyes, Luis Angel Salinas, Camilio Minero, and Noé Canjura—whose *Indian Christ* was purchased by the government of Guatemala. The works of all of these artists have been exhibited internationally. The best-known woman painter is Julia Díaz, who studied in Paris and whose works have been well received in the United States and Europe, as well as in a number of Latin American countries.

A crafts shop in Ilobasco illustrates that Salvadoran ceramics are brightly colored and intricate. The shapes of the vessels may have an ancient tradition, while the designs and ornamentation on plates and figures recall the country's mixed Indian-and-Spanish past.

The facade of the imposing Bascilica of San Salvador has a flamboyant Gothic flavor. The Catholic Church in El Salvador is an active participant in the dialogue to resolve civil strife, but has often been accused by the government of being pro-rebel. The archbishop of San Salvador has been instrumental in arranging talks between the representatives of the government and the FMLN.

## Religion

Four of five Salvadorans are Roman Catholics. The Church is taking an active role in the struggle for social justice and frequently criticizes the country's government. The Church is unable to staff all of its parishes from the local population. Presently, about half of El Salvador's parishes are served by foreign priests, many of whom are Italians and Spaniards belonging to international religious orders, chiefly the Salesians and the Jesuits. These foreign clerics, some from the United States, are often accused of meddling in domestic political affairs and of promoting political divisions among a nation whose basic desire is for peace.

Against this background, Protestant sects are making substantial headway in winning adherents because of their emphasis on good works and their refusal to be drawn into partisan politics. The Assemblies of God, the Seventh Day Adventists, the Church of God, and a few Pentecostal groups, all of which emphasize fundamentalist and participatory forms of worship, are attracting increasing numbers of Salvadorans. Baptists, too, are active in El Salvador with programs to help those whose lives have been disrupted by the fighting.

## Food

The diet of most Salvadorans is similar to that of other Latin Americans. A simple breakfast of coffee, rolls, and fruit suffices until lunch, the main meal, during which rice, corn, and beans are frequently eaten; less commonly seen are meat, poultry, and fish.

Dinners are somewhat lighter and often include a wider range of vegetables. Particularly in rural areas, the diet is heavy on starches and is often below minimum standards of caloric intake.

In metropolitan areas, the diet is more varied and often includes many foods processed by Salvadoran companies. For the

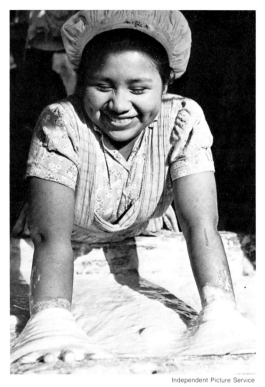

Independent Picture Service

Dough for tortillas, the thin, starchy cakes that are a Latin American staple, is kneaded by hand.

Courtesy of David Mangurian

An old market vendor proudly offers his fresh produce for sale.

49

At an inside grocery stall, women carefully choose from among the bright, ripe vegetables—carrots, cauliflower, cucumbers, and cabbage. El Salvador's warm climate produces a wide variety of fruits and vegetables.

Food vendors circumvent the need for stands and increase their mobility by purveying their wares to bus riders through open windows.

Courtesy of Earl H. Lubensky

On a festive religious holiday, Indians of the Izalco area in bright headdresses and colorful garments reenact a drama based on the European wars between the Spaniards and Moors—wars that took place 5,000 miles away and whose history was taught to the Indians' ancestors by Spanish priests in the sixteenth century.

well-to-do of San Salvador, there are supermarkets offering a broad range of products. The capital is internationally known for its many fine restaurants and for the excellence of its seafood, including shrimp, lobster, and swordfish caught in the Pacific.

The *pupusa*, a cornmeal cake stuffed with beans, bacon, cheese, and various spice leaves, is a national specialty. *Pupuserías*, shops that offer this delicacy, are widespread in both rural and urban areas of El Salvador.

## Festivals

El Salvador's most important national religious festival falls in the first week of August and venerates the Holy Savior of the World, after whom both the country and capital city were named. During this week, a wooden image of Christ, carved in 1777, is paraded through the streets of San Salvador to the National Palace and the cathedral, after which a band plays the national anthem.

The festival also includes special sports events—soccer games, bicycle races, and boxing matches. Operators of ferris wheels and merry-go-rounds do a thriving business at this time. A Queen of the August Fair is crowned by the provincial governor, and several downtown streets are closed to traffic so that folk artists can depict religious themes in dyed sawdust—much in the same manner that the Indians of the southwestern United States produce sand paintings.

In rural areas, each town and village has an annual celebration to honor its patron saint. These events may be lively affairs—with fireworks, band concerts, the breaking of *piñatas* (candy-filled papier-mâché figures), games, and, of course, religious ceremonies with as much pomp as can be arranged. These traditional celebrations and rituals have an important place in national life.

Photo by Charles Borniger

**President Duarte (*white shirt*) and military commanders tour a village damaged in the fighting between rebel and government troops. The amount of money spent to continue the conflict and to rebuild destroyed industries and services has dangerously burdened the Salvadoran economy.**

# 4) The Economy

The persistent civil war, depressed international commodity prices, and a loss of faith in future stability have combined to exact a heavy toll from the Salvadoran economy and to increase the number of Salvadorans seeking a better life in other lands. Between 1979 and 1982, when civil disruption was at its height, the value of the country's production of goods and services declined by 25 percent, and the value of exports decreased by 40 percent.

During that period, more than 100 factories closed their doors, and unemployment soared to a record 40 percent of the nation's labor force. Over the longer period, the picture was equally dismal. Per capita income in 1985 was the same as it was in 1960—a revealing statistic in a developing nation.

The Salvadoran government's total outlay for conducting the seven-year civil war is estimated to be well in excess of $1 billion—resources that might have been applied to satisfying the basic needs of the nation's population. From the rebel point of view, political instability and economic disruption are helpful factors in pursuing their cause. Roughly 10,000 rebels have severely damaged bridges, roads, and a costly hydroelectric plant and have interrupted vital power and communication services. To offset the exploitation of the situation by the insurgents and to prevent a possible Communist takeover of El Salvador, the Reagan administration contributed both money ($441 million in 1985) and military assistance (including U.S. military advisors). This aid is part of a U.S. effort to support Central American regimes fighting against Communist-backed rebel forces.

Because the production of coffee, cotton, sugar, and henequen (used in rope making) represents sizable investments and is so vital to the health of the Salvadoran economy, the country's armed forces—numbering 50,000 including police—have tried to protect these crops from guerrilla attack. To a large extent government troops have succeeded. The army is aided by the location of most of this commodity production on large, efficient landholdings in the central highlands or in the south—areas where the roads are good and the means of communication are advanced.

## Agriculture

Despite troubled times, agriculture remains the mainstay of the Salvadoran

Henequen, or sisal, is an important part of Salvadoran agricultural output. A worker changes the raw fiber into yarn that will later be used to produce rope, twine, or rough cloth.

economy with 52 percent of the economically active population engaged in farming. Even the guerrilla factions seeking to topple the government have avoided interfering with small holdings operated by *campesinos* because these peasant workers form the basis of their grassroots support.

The growing of sugarcane and cacao and the raising of cattle were introduced in colonial times. Coffee became El Salvador's leading cash crop after its introduction in the middle of the last century.

Under normal circumstances, coffee is still El Salvador's main source of foreign earnings in world trade and accounts for 78 percent of the value of its exports. The country ordinarily depends on the sale of its high-quality coffee crop to provide the money to pay for many essential imports, including machinery, vehicles, pharmaceuticals, and foodstuffs, mainly from the United States, Western Europe, and Japan.

Coffee is grown on roughly 320,000 acres in the highlands. The small coffee trees are planted in the shade of taller trees. With their glossy dark green leaves and bright red berries, coffee plants have an attractive appearance.

Cotton is cultivated on some 130,000 acres in the southern coastal plains and represents about 16 percent of the value

On a large *finca* (plantation), coffee beans are spread out to dry on a stone terrace called a drying platform. The bean-yielding trees were introduced to El Salvador in the middle of the nineteenth century and have since become the nation's main agricultural export. Coffee growing is still a tricky and time-consuming business; it demands good weather and careful production methods. Most trees are planted in mountainous areas.

Faced with a huge mound of plucked cotton, a boy and his father begin the tedious job of filling sacks, which are made of rough-woven sisal fiber.

of total exports. Yields of both cotton and coffee per acre are among the highest in the world.

About 65,000 acres are planted in sugar-cane. Cane production is of two kinds—large-scale, efficient plantations supplying modern sugar mills with cane for processing for the export market, and small, inefficient plots turning out cane that is converted into crude, dark, loaf sugar, called *panela*.

El Salvador's pronounced wet and dry seasons render the lowlands unsuitable for regular planting because of the alternating floods and droughts. Therefore, much of these lands and the Lempa River Valley are used for grazing livestock rather than for growing food.

## Subsistence Farming

In terms of the number of Salvadorans for whom agriculture provides a living, the most important single economic activity

In Cihuatán, a campesino hitches his oxen as he prepares to begin the back-breaking work of plowing his small field.

A fertile field of sugarcane that overlooks the hills of El Salvador will produce the sugar eventually exported to international markets.

A comparison of a large, flat sugarcane field (*above*) and a small, hilly, rock-filled plot belonging to an average campesino (*left*) emphasizes the disparity of land distribution between rich and poor. Government efforts to mount an effective agrarian-reform program, mostly inspired by U.S. demands, have stagnated in recent years.

is peasant subsistence farming. Campesinos cultivate small, rented plots, where they produce maize, beans, sorghum, and rice for their own consumption. For the most part, their harvests do not enter the cash economy, though the farmers may barter or trade small quantities in village and town markets to obtain other essentials. These homegrown foods, produced on plots rarely exceeding 30 or 40 acres, provide an amount barely sufficient to sustain human life and constitute a diet often inadequate in nutritional value.

## Land Reform

Inequity in the division of land is a prime cause of insurrection in El Salvador. Four percent of the landowners own 60 percent of the land. Fewer than half of 1 percent of the total number of farms is spread over 35 percent of the most fertile land. Peasant farming—often on poor quality soil located on steep and rocky hillsides—makes up by far the largest sector of the Salvadoran economy but occupies less than 17 percent of the land under cultivation.

Belatedly, and under pressure from the United States, the government of El Salvador passed landmark legislation in 1980 that intended to dismantle large landholdings and redistribute them to land-hungry peasants through a carefully phased program.

The initial phase transferred holdings of greater than 1,235 acres from landowners to cooperatives, which are composed of farmers who had once worked the same land as farm laborers. Another phase in the redistribution program sold small parcels of land (about 17 acres) to individual farmers and their families. These two phases of land reform transferred nearly 800,000 acres to over half a million farmers and family members.

Despite the redistribution of so much land to needful Salvadorans, major difficulties have plagued the program. Landowners strongly resisted—sometimes

A farmer leads his donkey through a field of sorghum— one of the main subsistence crops.

Near Usulután, a large field has been plowed to the contour of the land to prevent soil erosion. Owners of sizable holdings can afford advanced technology—another inequality between rich and poor farmers.

violently—giving up their large holdings. Cooperative farms accumulated heavy debts because of poor financial planning at the outset of reform efforts in 1979 and 1980. Farm owners of small parcels of land often did not receive the technical assistance that would have increased crop productivity.

Considerable work still remains to make a success of El Salvador's land-reform initiatives. The hope for the program is twofold—that ownership of land by a much larger population of Salvadorans will weaken the powerful political relationship between the army and the few wealthy landowners, and that an increasing number of family incomes will rise well above the poverty level.

## Manufacturing

Up until the outbreak of war with Honduras in 1969, El Salvador had pinned high hopes on its ability to expand its manufacturing capacity and to provide more jobs in industry. During the 1960s, the country was helped greatly by its membership in the Central American Common Market (CACM). Salvadoran entrepreneurs were enthusiastic participants in this arrangement, which enabled their

Juana Petrona Nieto, a biologist who works for the Center for Agricultural Technology in San Andrés, checks yellow corn seeds to determine whether their high germination rate and general characteristics are sufficiently advanced to certify the seeds for sale to farmers.

country's businesspersons to develop industries that could sell products and services within the five-nation CACM area.

Industrias Unidas, a textile plant, employs nearly 2,000 people and produces 850,000 pounds of thread and 1.5 million yards of cotton, polyester, and blended fabrics every month, mostly for sale abroad. The plant is one of the largest manufacturing concerns in Central America and is a joint venture of Salvadoran and Japanese businesspersons.

For a few years, there was optimism and confidence on the streets of San Salvador. University students demonstrated in favor of regional unity; postage stamps proudly proclaimed, "Centroamérica" (Central America); products were labeled, "Hecho en Centroamérica" (Made in Central America).

Business boomed as El Salvador capitalized on the quintupling of trade within the common market area. With foreign investment and technology, food processing—including canning and freezing homegrown crops and processing locally harvested beans into instant coffee—became the most important industry. The textile industry, producing clothes from Salvadoran cotton, came in second place.

As the expanded market provided more consumers, El Salvador developed its production of chemicals, petroleum derivatives, insecticides and fungicides, organic fertilizers, soaps, paints, varnishes, plastics, and pharmaceuticals. These new items complemented the well-established manufacture and distribution of beverages. Beer,

Foreign investments in the 1970s and 1980s produced a wave of building and industrial development. Construction workers on the government-financed San Lorenzo hydroelectric project have good reason to smile—they are paid more than the minimum wage.

A kiln located in San Salvador produces bricks for home building and is an example of a small business run by members of one family.

liquor, and soft drinks were brewed, distilled, and bottled in quantities greater than the local demand and were sold within Central America. There was increased demand for cement and construction materials to accommodate the domestic housing boom. Consequently, production of furniture and home fixtures to appoint the new dwellings also rose.

## Transportation

As a compact country, El Salvador has one of the best-developed systems of land transport in all of Latin America. The Pan-American Highway links all major Salvadoran cities, and secondary motorways connect the towns of the country. Until roads were damaged during the civil war, it was possible to travel from San Salvador

Courtesy of Inter-American Development Bank

The José Simeón Cañas Urban Center on the outskirts of San Salvador has 140 high-rise buildings with 13,000 apartment units, together with schools, shops, and community facilities—not to mention a view of of San Salvador Volcano in the distance.

The municipal bus system in San Salvador is inadequate for the number of people who use it. Public conveyances are often overloaded, with riders hanging on wherever they can find something to grab.

A section of railway track passes through a grove of bamboo trees. Though crowded, the trains offer a window-seat view of El Salvador's varied landscape.

to any border of the country within a few hours. The number of vehicles using the road system is currently about 140,000 and doubles every 10 years. There are, however, few roads within the rugged mountainous areas. There, travel must be accomplished by tough four-wheel-drive vehicles, on horse or mule, or on foot.

San Salvador's new airport, Cuscatlán, is located at La Libertad, about 20 miles from the capital. It is a modern facility that serves travelers bound for international destinations. Because of El Salvador's small size and good road system, it has not developed a network of regularly scheduled domestic air transportation.

A railway system with approximately 400 miles of track provides service from San Salvador to the eastern port of La Unión on the Gulf of Fonseca and west to the port of Acajutla; this line eventually

Workers maintain part of the Pan-American Highway in western El Salvador, which is part of the vital road network over which much of the country's commerce passes.

crosses the border and runs to Guatemala City. Trains are often slow and passenger accommodations primitive, but there is rewarding scenery along all routes.

## Communications

The government operates the telephone, telegraph, and mail systems. Within El Salvador, the telephone system is badly overloaded. Telephones are hard to obtain, and calls are often difficult because of shortages of switchboard connections. Improvements in the use of satellites have meant that international calling, to the United States for example, is often easier than calling by land connections to much closer locations in neighboring countries.

Television was first introduced in 1956 and has experienced rapid growth. There are now three commercial television chan-

nels and a government-operated educational channel. El Salvador has 39 radio stations; most of them are located in the San Salvador area, but 4 reach a national audience. The capital city has four daily newspapers, whose position on El Salvador's political situation has sometimes depended on the strength or weakness of the government in power.

Newsstands offer a wide selection of foreign periodicals; many are publications in Spanish originating from Mexico. The government and universities publish a few books each year. This provides an outlet for intellectuals, though many Salvadoran writers choose to issue their works through foreign publishing firms.

## Workers and Social Welfare

The Salvadoran wage scale is determined

Only since 1983 have labor movements flourished in El Salvador, making it possible for workers to meet with their union representatives to discuss the important issues of wages and working conditions.

by occupation; most workers are poorly paid. Farm workers receive less than industrial workers, but neither group gets very much. There has been little success in organizing the Salvadoran labor force to achieve better conditions because of governmental opposition and oligarchical resistance.

Trade unions were illegal until 1950. Now there is an official code that strictly regulates union activity, controlling collective bargaining and limiting the right to strike. The code does provide some benefits like minimum wages, paid vacations, and restrictions on the hours of work.

Despite obstacles, Salvadoran workers are actively involved in promoting their rights. During the May Day celebration of 1986, 20,000 workers marched through the capital city—some carrying rebel banners—to demonstrate labor's discontent with working conditions. Targets of complaint included a government-sponsored social security system that has failed to reach a majority of the country's workers, mainly because few employers comply with the program's regulations. These call for employers to register their employees and to contribute to the system

an amount equal to 5 percent of worker earnings.

Today, there are two principal union organizations—the General Confederation of Unions with 27,000 members, which represents about two-thirds of those workers who are organized, and the largely Communist General Confederation of Salvadoran Workers with 3,500 members. Most of the 93 trade unions are small— only 2 have more than 1,000 members. Fewer than 6 percent of all of El Salvador's wage earners and salaried workers are organized, and such organization extends no further than the urban areas.

Unemployment in El Salvador remains high. With civil strife, few new jobs are being created to accommodate young Salvadorans who are entering the nation's labor force. Thousands of Salvadorans have joined the growing tide of legal and illegal immigration into the United States. Although the earnings these refugees send home have become an important source of income for El Salvador, the country has been drained of many of its most highly motivated and most intelligent young people—a serious loss for a country in need of all its natural and human resources.

**63**

# Index